Red Herring Mysteries
Level 1
Solving Mysteries Through Critical Questioning

SERIES TITLES

Red Herring Mysteries - Level 1
Red Herring Mysteries - Level 2

Written By
Thomas Camilli

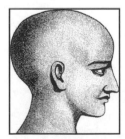

© 2007
THE CRITICAL THINKING CO.™
(BRIGHT MINDS™)
Phone: 800-458-4849 Fax: 831-393-3277
www.CriticalThinking.com
P.O. Box 1610 • Seaside • CA 93955-1610
ISBN 978-1-60144-162-1

Printed in the United States of America

TABLE OF CONTENTS

About This Book

The activities in this book are designed to improve your students' problem solving skills and refine their ability to apply logical deductive reasoning. To accomplish these, students are given the opportunity to solve puzzling mysteries in much the same way as a real detective—by asking probing questions and forming conclusions based upon the answers.

These activities can also help to change the way your students think. For example, the solution to some of the mysteries may require students to alter stereotyped sex roles or recognize the multiple meanings of key words.

How It Works

Each of the "mysteries" on these pages is part of a longer untold story which is "behind the scenes." It is up to the students to deduce the rest of the story from clues derived from answers to their questions.

For example, the story behind the sentence, "If Leo had kept his hand down he might be a free man today," can eventually be revealed if enough questions are asked and the answers are used to form a mental image of the event.

It may take many questions over several days to finally reveal that Leo is a not-too-bright bank robber who incriminates himself at his trial by raising his hand when the prosecutor asks a witness, "Is the person who robbed the bank present in the courtroom today?"

The Rules of the Game

The rules for these activities are simple.

• Students must phrase their questions so that the answer is either yes or no.

• You should try to answer questions with only a yes or no (occasionally a maybe or sometimes can be given as an appropriate response).

• You may give hints to redirect thinking or stimulate new questions.

Behind the Scenes

The solutions to these mysteries are found at the back of this book. It is important to visualize the scenario of the mystery before you begin a questioning session. That way you can answer questions based upon your personal mental image of what has taken place. After visualizing the scene, you may find that you need to alter it slightly to suit your geographic locale or your students' cultural backgrounds.

Suggestions for Use

As a motivator or time filler: These detective mysteries can be used as five-minute warm-up or sponge activities to begin or end a class period.

As a cooperative activity: Students can be divided into teams. Limiting the number of questions that a team is allowed to ask keeps one group from dominating the session. Each team may ask only one question per round, and the questions may be asked only by the team's spokesperson. This helps to eliminate frivolous questions. (In fact, many students will learn quickly how to narrow the search for important clues by asking comprehensive questions.)

Another method for limiting questioning is to pass out coupons to the groups before each session. A coupon is collected before each question is answered. When the group runs out of coupons, the group is out of that questioning session.

As a writing activity: Questions may be submitted only in writing. Questions are read and answered at the beginning or end of class. To prevent students who already know the answer from spoiling the activity for others, possible solutions should also be submitted only in writing.

To develop critical listening skills: After a few practice rounds, a new rule could be imposed: repeat questions will not be answered. This causes students to listen more carefully to each other's questions and answers.

Critical listening and recall is improved if the students are allowed to remark (with a noise or a word) when a question is a repeat of one that has already been asked.

As a lesson in critical thinking: Like all good mystery stories, the ones in this book have vivid plots, settings, and characters. Questioning strategies can be improved by finding areas of the stories that have not been thoroughly addressed. By analyzing individual questions and suggesting ways to improve them, you can increase students' critical thinking ability.

Tips

- Limiting the number of questions allowed during a session tends to improve the quality of the questions.

- Choosing a student to present the story and answer the questions allows you to model inquiry techniques by taking an active part in the activity. Instead of simply describing how to formulate good questions, you can then guide the students by demonstrating higher level thinking and questioning techniques.

- It is important to summarize the clues that have already been discovered before continuing an interrupted questioning session. This refreshes students' memories and updates students who may have been absent during a questioning session. One of the best ways to do this is to ask the students what they remember about the story and what clues have already been revealed.

Using the Mystery Pages

The pages in this book are designed for multiple uses.

- Reproducing the mystery page on transparency material and using it every time the story is investigated helps students who have a limited auditory memory.

- Summarizing what the students already know about the mystery and writing it on the transparency will help those students with learning difficulties to continue to participate in the questioning activity.

- Letting everyone see the actual mystery message permits students to analyze the wording of the mystery for possible clues.

- Using the mystery page as a poster in your room will serve to remind you and your students of both the activity and the mystery in progress.

Using the Graphic Organizers

A variety of graphic organizers could be used to help students with the thinking process. Two are supplied with this text. Here are some ways that they can be used:

For cooperative learning: Before beginning the questioning session, each group receives one copy of the mystery story and a copy of the graphic organizers. Encourage them to use the graphic organizers to arrange a questioning strategy. At the end of the session the group members can map out on the organizer the direction in which the answers are leading and plan the next questioning strategies.

Modeling the thinking process: Using a transparency of Organizer #1, select a mystery and model the process of analyzing the story for clues. Are there any words in the story that could have multiple meanings? Are there any clues about the setting, characters, or action of the story? From the first reading of the mystery, what are some possible solutions?

Guided practice: Individually or in cooperative groups, students could use Organizer #1 to help them analyze the wording of a mystery story. They could contribute their ideas about the mystery before beginning the questioning session.

Summarizing: Organizer #2 can be used to list the clues that have been discovered from previous questioning sessions.

The Questioning Process

To give you a better understanding of how to use these mystery stories to develop critical thinking, here is an abbreviated script of a questioning session with a group of students.

The teacher in this example uses several strategies to get the students to think in new and different directions without giving away the premise of the story. You might want to use similar strategies with your students to get them back on track if they get stuck or start pursuing a nonproductive line of questioning.

Teacher: "We're going to try to solve a mystery today. I know the entire story behind this mystery, but I am only going to let you begin with a small part of it. It will be up to you to figure out the rest of the story as a detective would, by asking good questions, listening carefully to the answers, and putting clues together to form a mental picture of what is happening.

"Here are some rules that must be followed. You may ask me any question as long as it is phrased so that my answer can be a yes or a no. Listen to the questions that others ask because you may pick up clues from my answers to their questions. Try not to repeat questions that others have already asked.

"I will attempt to answer your questions with only a yes or a no. Sometimes that is difficult to do, so I may give more than a one-word answer to some questions. Listen to the way that I answer yes or no. That may give you a clue to the solution of the mystery or help you phrase your next question.

"Do you understand the rules? If not, be sure to ask for an explanation. OK, here is the mystery story: (the teacher places the transparency of the story on the overhead). It reads, 'Although she was not an unusually large person, people were constantly amazed at what Livia weighed.'"

Student: "What do you mean? Who is she? Is she really a big person?"

Teacher: "That's what you are supposed to find out by asking questions. If you ask enough questions, you can find out exactly what is happening here. Try it. Remember, your questions must be phrased so that I can answer them with yes or no."

Student: "Who is she?"

Teacher: "I can't answer that question the way it is asked. Please rephrase the question so that I can answer it with a yes or a no."

Student: "Is she a person?"

Teacher: "Yes. That's a good question. Why do you think it is a good question?"

Student: "The word she could mean lots of things. It could stand for an animal, like a lioness. Sometimes ships are called she."

Student: "When the story says that people were constantly amazed at what she weighed, does that mean that she was a really large person?"

Teacher: "No one said that she was a large person. You have to listen carefully to the way the story is told for clues to the mystery. Now, how is the story worded? Read it carefully because every word counts."

Student: "How can she be a small person and still weigh a lot—enough that people were amazed at her?"

Teacher: "I can't answer until your thought is posed as a question."

Student: "Is she a weight lifter? Does she compete in the Olympics?"

Teacher: "That's two questions. I can only answer one at a time."

Student: "OK, is Livia a weight lifter?"

Teacher: "No."

Student: "Does this have anything to do with how many pounds she weighs?"

Teacher: "No. Good question."

Student: "Does weigh mean that she weighs things for other people, you know like a butcher weighs meat for other people?"

Teacher: "No."

Student: "Does she weigh big things, like trucks or elephants?"

Teacher: "No."

Student: "Does the word weigh have anything to do with finding the mass of an object?"

Teacher: "No. But why is that a good question?"

Student: "It eliminates a lot of things with just one question."

Student: "Is Livia a judge?"

Teacher: "Before I answer your question, what made you think of that?"

Student: "Well, judges sometimes have to weigh the evidence in a case to reach a decision."

Teacher: "That's good thinking. Another use for the word weigh. I'm sorry, but the answer is no. Did that question start any of you thinking in a different direction?"

Student: "Yes, it makes me see that words can have more than one meaning."

Student: "Would it help to know what Livia does for a living?"

Teacher: "Yes."

Student: "Does Livia drive a truck?"

Teacher: "No."

Student: "Is she an airline pilot?"

Teacher: "No. Can you think of some questions that could narrow down what she does without having to go through all the occupations in the world?"

Student: "Does she work indoors?"

Teacher: "That's a good question. It covers a whole group of occupations with one question. The answer is no."

Student: "Can we then assume that she works outdoors?"

Teacher: "A good detective never assumes anything. They question every assumption to get at the truth."

Student: "Does Livia work outdoors?"

Teacher: "Yes."

Student: "Does she work on land?"

Teacher: "No."

Student: "Does she work at sea?"

Teacher: "Yes."

Student: "Does she work on a ship?"

Teacher: "Yes."

Student: "Oh, I think I know the answer!"

Teacher: "If you think you know, ask a question that will help others to discover the answer."

Student: "Does Livia work mostly when the ship enters and leaves port?"

Teacher: "Yes."

Student: "Does the word weigh have something to do with a part of the ship?"

Teacher: "Yes. I think you are close to the solution. Ask another question"

Student: "Is Livia in charge of raising and lowering the anchor on a ship?"

Teacher: "Yes. That's it!"

Student: "Huh?"

Teacher: "Livia handles the controls that raise and lower the massive anchor on the ship. She weighs it. In this case, the word weigh means to raise something. Can you see how people would be constantly amazed at what Livia weighed?

"Now, do you think you understand how these mystery stories work? Well, here's another one for you to try to solve. If we don't have time to complete it today, we'll work on it when we have some time left over tomorrow or the next day."

Levels of Difficulty

The mystery stories in this book have been leveled according to the amount of difficulty students will have reaching the solution. The stories in the beginning of the book are easier for the average class to deduce than those farther back. The first two or three stories are excellent to use when modelling the questioning process needed to solve the remainder of the mysteries.

Many stories in the last third of this book are complicated and will require a much longer period of time to solve. You may have to give more clues and actively guide your students' thinking as they work through some of the more difficult mystery stories.

Extending Activities

After students have experience solving the mysteries in this book, ask them to create their own stories. Sources for story ideas are mystery programs on television and unusual stories from magazines, mystery novels, or the newspaper.

The best mysteries are those which contain

words that have more than one meaning. For example, a story could be one floor in a tall building, or it could be a written or spoken composition. A stroke could have something to do with the brain, or it could be a term that describes a tennis or golf swing. Try to incorporate these kinds of words into the story.

Mystery Story: _____

_____

_____

Words in the story which have multiple meanings:

Word: _____ Meanings: _____

Word: _____ Meanings: _____

Word: _____ Meanings: _____

Word: _____ Meanings: _____

What clues can you find in the words of the mystery story?

Setting clues	Character clues	Action clues
_____	_____	_____
_____	_____	_____
_____	_____	_____
_____	_____	_____
_____	_____	_____
_____	_____	_____
_____	_____	_____

Possible Solutions:

_____

_____

_____

_____

_____

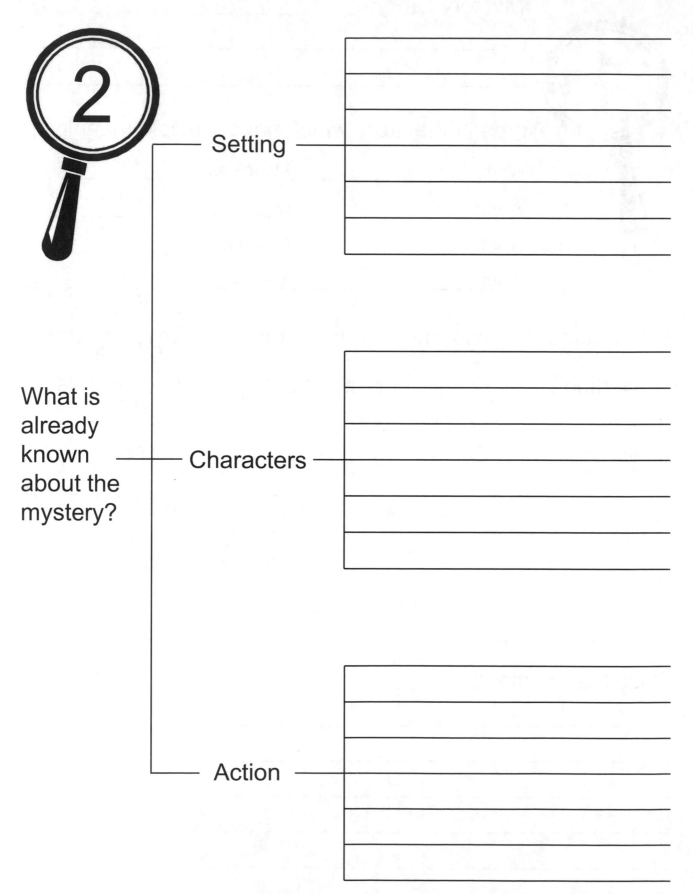

What is already known about the mystery?

Setting

Characters

Action

Tana announced to her colleagues that she had created something that has no beginning, no end, and nothing in the middle. If they would stop by in the morning, she would share the formula for her creation with them. They did and she did. What did she create?

There were no hits, most of the pitches were either too low or too high, and none of the players on either side knew the score. Yet the stands were full and the crowd cheered with excitement.

How can that be?

The high school's water polo team was always doing unusual things.

Once they stayed in a pool for an entire game without anyone on the team getting wet.

How did they do it?

While on his way to the museum with some friends, Manuel tripped and fell over forty feet.

He survived his ordeal without so much as a scratch or a bruise.

How was this possible?

A woman put on a heavy coat and left home for the rest of the day.

It was neither raining nor cold outside.

Why would she do this?

Even though anesthetized, the dental patient started moaning loudly as the drilling began. Later the moans turned to screams of pain. The dentist seemed unconcerned by this action and later thanked the patient for her cries of anguish. Why?

Relentlessly pursued by an opposing army, he suddenly found that he had nowhere to run or hide.

Two baseball teams were in the playoffs for the championships. They played five games and each team won the same number of games. How is that possible?

What occurs in the middle of each month, in every season except summer, and happens in nighttime, but never in daylight?

Stanley praised the opportunities America provided immigrants. "When I came to this country," he said, "I knew only two words of English, but that didn't stop me from making my fortune." What does Stanley do and what were the two words of English that he knew?

Although it was not very heavy, nobody on board the ship could hold it for more than a few minutes. What was it?

A world famous French chef unexpectedly quit her job at a fashionable restaurant.

When asked her reason for quitting, the chef replied through an interpreter, "I just can't stand to cook anymore."

What could be wrong?

A scientist announced that he had discovered the ability to travel backwards or forwards in time.

In front of the media and hundreds of witnesses, he proved his claim.

Up against the wall,
he knew it was all over.

One afternoon, while camping with her family, Bev was asked to go to the river and bring back a bucket full of water.

To her surprise, the only bucket she could find had several large holes in its bottom.

Undismayed, Bev managed to fulfill the request. How did she do it?

While strolling through the park one evening, Hiroshi noticed a large crowd of people gathered around two men who were obviously fighting.

Both men had knives and were slashing furiously at each other. Although there were policemen present, nobody attempted to stop the fight. Why?

The sign outside the business reads, "If you don't come in we will both starve."

What kind of business is it?

When asked what he does for a living, Hans says that he just sits around all day making faces. What does Hans do?

Although she was not an unusually large woman, people were always surprised at what Livia weighed.

After an invigorating walk in the park, Alex returned home to find two fierce looking women waiting for her. Although one of the women appeared quite angry, Alex was not the least bit disturbed by their presence. Why?

Although Gwen's parents often were not happy with her use of foul language, they were powerless to stop her from using it in front of them and their friends.

Why?

Bubba "Fingers" Bronkowitz recently retired after playing twenty years for the Salina Sluggers.

During his entire career he never missed a game, yet he never once wore the team's uniform.

How can that be?

A generous aunt, tired of never receiving thank you notes from her ungrateful nephews, decided to do something about it. As a result of her plan, her nephews stopped by to personally thank her for her gift. What did she do?

Joey the Lip boasted to his pals that he had thought up a way to quickly make a lot of crooked dough. The best part of it was that nobody had ever thought up this scheme before and nobody would be able to use it without his "poisonal OK." What was Joey's scheme?

The driver of a public works' truck was exhibiting unusual behavior.

The man would stop the truck alongside the road every twenty feet, get out, and dig a hole. He would wait exactly five minutes and then fill the hole in, tamping the dirt with his foot.

Why was he doing this?

Although they had continually lowered the prices all morning, the members of a high school club could get no one to stop for their Saturday car wash.

Then one student hit upon a brilliant idea that brought them more business and raised more money than any previous car wash ever had.

What did the student do?

Theresa was a volunteer in a scientific experiment.

Although she hadn't slept for four days, medical tests showed that she wasn't the least bit tired.

How could that be?

Told that he would be granted one final request, the condemned man asked to be allowed to sing his favorite song one last time.

His request effectively spared his life. How?

An airline passenger needed to transport a delicate item on the plane with him. The item was too large to fit in the overhead compartment or under the seat in front of him. If it was checked as luggage, it would surely be crushed.

Faced with the dilemma, the man creatively solved his problem. What did he do?

A student stopped by a music store wanting to buy an accessory for his musical instrument. When he saw the price of the accessory, he knew that he couldn't afford it, so he left.

The next day he returned and paid cash for the accessory. How did he get the money?

Antonia was outstanding in her field. When reporters asked what started her on the road to success, she would answer that a lot of it had to do with her ability to raise wheat, corn, and strawberries.

Many people were amused by her remark. Why?

The sign outside a business reads, "If you don't see what you want, you've come to the right place."

What kind of business is it?

A husband and wife celebrated their 25th birthdays with their nine children, twenty grandchildren, and six great-grandchildren. How can that be?

Although she had lots of friends and had made millions of dollars during her long and successful career, Alise suddenly found herself alone and penniless. How can that be?

A massive earthquake destroys a dam at the mouth of a huge reservoir. Although a large community is in the direct path of floodwaters, no homes are destroyed or people killed. How can that be?

If only she had seen the light, she might be free today. What happened?

Jen told her friends that what she does for a living takes strength, skill, patience, determination, and lots of guts. What does she do?

Although a wealthy woman, Elsa only made friends with the poor and destitute. Why?

An inventor informed the press that he had devised a way to jump higher than the roof of his laboratory building without the aid of any mechanical device. When the news media arrived to document the event, they were surprised by what they saw. What was that?

While on an outing with some friends, twin sisters ate identical meals prepared by the same person. One of the twins remained perfectly healthy while the other became critically ill after the meal. Why?

The sign read, "We may be whipped, but we will never be beaten." Where is the sign, and what is meant by it?

Although the woman deliberately jumped from the top of the tallest building in town, she was neither injured nor killed by the fall. How can that be?

Lavar knew that for what he had done, he would eventually have to face the music. Why?

It is found in England, France, Spain, and China, but not in Portugal, Italy, or Greece. What is it?

The car traveled for nearly a mile with a flat tire, yet the driver was unaware of it. How can that be?

Two identical containers are each filled with the same food, yet one container weighs substantially less than the other container. How can that be?

Working together, two shoplifters stole something from a store. As a result, they each received six months for their crime. What did they steal?

Even though he made straight A's in school, Louis was not allowed to graduate with his class. Why?

"Sharks! Sharks!" shouted the lifeguard, but none of the swimmers seemed the least bit concerned for their safety. Why?

If she hadn't crossed
the line, they might both
be alive today. What
happened?

A heavily armed man held up a series of bars, robbing onlookers of their gold and silver. Although many of the onlookers knew the identity of the man, the police were never notified of the incidents. Why?

A woman found herself jailed for stopping her car before turning right at a busy intersection. How can that be?

Even though his face was completely masked throughout the robbery, police were waiting for him when he arrived at his home. How did they know?

The sign outside the business read, "Don't jump to conclusions. Take your time, pack carefully, and read and follow all directions." What was the business?

She had captivated the crowd with her performance, but she knew disenchantment would quickly follow the next strike. What is happening?

Ludlow got detention for asking to have his spelling corrected. How can that be?

When they invented it, they never realized how many lives it would save. What is it?

I live in a strange town. The law states that no man may shave himself. Instead, every man must be shaved by the town barber. But there is only one barber in town. Who shaves the barber?

While peeling potatoes for dinner, Mac accidentally cut his finger. Within a few minutes he was dead. What happened?

The headline read, "Woman Survives Twenty Story Fall." How could she have done that?

After both engines failed, the pilot ordered the passengers and crew to bail out. Even though not a single parachute opened, they all survived the ordeal. How?

Taking advantage of a momentary distraction caused by her companions, she broke free from the guards and fled in a futile attempt to evade capture. Why was she being held?

Within the space of a week she had married and divorced two men and was engaged to marry another, yet those who knew her were not surprised by her actions. Why?

The headline read, "Unexpected Plant Closure Surprises Workers." What is the story about?

BEHIND THE SCENES

1. Tana had just cooked up her first batch of doughnuts (bagels will also work)—an object with no beginning, no end, and nothing in the middle. She gave her colleagues each a doughnut (or bagel) and the recipe (formula) for making them.

2. The crowd was a group of eager parents attending the first concert of a beginning band. Although the music stands were full of sheet music, the unskilled orchestra members couldn't play anything recognizable.

3. The pool was a car pool that the team formed to get to their matches. In this case, they were watching a game between two other teams.

4. Manuel was going to the museum with his school class. As the last to board the bus, he tripped and fell over many of the outspread feet of his classmates as he made his way to his seat in the back.

5. The woman was painting her house. She put a heavy coat of paint on the interior walls and then left the house until the paint had a chance to dry.

6. The dentist wanted to leave early for a vacation trip, but there was one patient left in the waiting room. The dentist asked the patient in the chair, an actress, to demonstrate her acting skills by moaning and screaming as if in agony. The woman's anguish caused the waiting patient to reschedule his appointment, exactly what the dentist had hoped would happen.

7. He was the king in a game of chess. The player's opponent had just put the player's king in checkmate. The king was not safe where he was and could not move without being captured. The game is over.

8. The teams were in different leagues and didn't play each other.

9. The letter N.

10. Stanley is head of a crime family in a large American city. He began his infamous career by robbing people on the street. The two English words that he knew when he came to America were "hands up!"

11. Their breath. The people on the ship were all scuba divers who were testing how long they could hold their breath if they were ever forced to do it underwater.

12. The chef explained that because she had broken both of her legs in a skiing accident, she would no longer be able to do her job which required her to move about the restaurant kitchen. The interpreter summarized her statement and left out a few key parts of it.

13. The scientist realized that he could travel backwards in time a full day by crossing eastward over the international dateline. He could travel forwards in time a full day by crossing the international dateline in a westward direction.

   He invited the media and his friends to accompany him on a chartered voyage to do just that.

14. He was an outfielder in a baseball game. It was the bottom of the ninth inning. The score was tied, and there were two outs.

The person at bat hit a fly ball deep to the outfield. The outfielder jumped for the ball as it soared over the wall, but missed. The game was over and the other team was the winner.

15. Undismayed, Bev managed to fulfill the request. How did she do it?

Bev's family was camping in the middle of winter. Bev realized that it didn't matter if the bucket had holes in it since she was going to be filling it with ice from the frozen river.

16. Hiroshi stopped to watch a scene from a play that was being presented in the park. The seats were set up in such a way that the actors were in the center of the audience. Police were present to provide security for the production.

17. A restaurant.

18. Hans works in a factory that makes grandfather clocks. It is his job to create the beautiful designs that are on the faces of the clocks.

19. Livia works on a cruise ship and it is her job to lower and raise the anchor. Weighing anchor is another term for raising it.

20. The park is a baseball park and Alexandra (nicknamed Alex) is a player on an all-girl team who is on third base. The bases are loaded and the pitcher has just walked the person at bat. Alex gets to walk to home plate and score a run without the fear of being tagged out by the angry catcher.

21. Gwen is a referee for professional basketball. Gwen's parents are avid basketball fans and never miss a game that Gwen is refereeing. There are times, however, that they do not agree with her foul calls and let her know about it after the game. Their displeasure does not prevent Gwen from doing her job as fairly as she can.

22. Bubba was the team's organist. He played the National Anthem before each game.

23. The aunt sent each nephew slightly less than half of a one-hundred dollar bill. In order to spend the money, each nephew needed the other part of the bill. They paid her a personal visit.

24. Joey, who had been raised in a tough part of the inner city, was addressing a group of potential investors in his newly patented machine which produced pretzels (crooked dough) faster than any other machine in existence.

25. The man worked for the highway beautification division. He was part of a two-person tree planting crew. His partner, the one who actually plants the tree in the hole, was out sick that day.

26. The students belonged to the high school psychology club. After discussing what they knew about human nature, the students changed the sign to read, "FREE CAR WASH! DONATIONS ACCEPTED," knowing that people would rather donate to a worthy cause than be charged for a service. It worked.

27. She slept at night.

28. After being granted his request, the condemned man began singing, "Ten million bottles of beer on the wall...."

29. The man was transporting a delicate antique lamp shade. He hit upon the idea of wearing the lamp shade as a hat during the trip. It worked.

30. He had gone to the music store to buy a mute for his trumpet. When he saw that he couldn't afford one, he devised a plan.

    He went back to his apartment and began practicing with his unmuted trumpet. A sign on his door explained his predicament. His neighbors donated the money.

31. Antonia is a popular model and actress. She was discovered while appearing on cereal commercials. Her job in the commercial was to eat a bowl of wheat and corn flakes with cut strawberries in it. Reporters who had known her when she was appearing in the cereal commercials chuckled at her pun.

32. The business is the office of an optometrist.

33. The husband and wife were married to each other. They were both born on February 29, a leap day. Their birthdays technically happen only once every four years. Although they are both actually 100 years old, they are celebrating only their 25th birthdays.

34. Alise found herself alone and penniless in her cell in a federal prison. As a skilled forger, she had literally "made" millions of dollars in counterfeit money and now was being punished for her crime.

35. The area had been suffering from a prolonged drought, and as a result the reservoir was nearly empty when the dam collapsed.

36. Driving through a residential neighborhood late at night, a woman was stopped by the police for driving with a broken headlight. A check revealed that the car she was driving was not hers. It had been stolen earlier in the day and used in a series of bank robberies, and the woman had been the get-away driver. She was incarcerated for her crime.

37. Jen strings tennis rackets for professional tennis players. The special string used on professional rackets is called *gut*.

38. As a youngster, Elsa had heard the old saying that, "a friend in need is a friend indeed." Being a literal thinker, she believed it and practiced it in her daily life.

39. It had been a slow day. The inventor thought up a little joke to play on the media. It was easy for him to jump higher than the roof of his laboratory building since the roof of his laboratory building cannot jump at all. When the media arrived, they were greeted by a sign describing the hoax.

40. The twins were attending a community gathering in a local park. They had been stopping at various booths to sample food. At one booth they purchased a meal of cooked meat strips on wooden skewers. Unknown to them, the cook was running out of bamboo skewers and was cooking some of the meat on skewers made from the branches of a nearby bush. The wood contained a powerful toxin. One of the twin's meals was skewered on bamboo while the other's was cooked on poisonous branches.

41. The sign is part of an advertising campaign for a very proud dairy company.

42. Although she was neither injured nor killed by the fall, the woman was killed by the sudden stop at the end of the fall.

43. Lavar had recently graduated from a school of music and was embarking on a career as an orchestra conductor.

44. It is the letter N. It is also found in Japan, Canada, and Denmark.

45. The tire was on a new car that was being transported by truck, along with several other new cars, to an auto dealership.

46. Both containers are filled with popcorn. One is filled with the dried popcorn kernels, and the other is filled with popped corn.

47. A calendar.

48. Although Louis, a talented kindergarten student, made straight A's, his B's and C's were awful, and he didn't know how to write his other letters and numbers. As a result, he was required to repeat kindergarten.

49. The Sharks, the name of the visiting water polo team, had just scored a goal. The lifeguard for the event, also acting as the referee, was verifying the score by shouting the scoring team's name to the scorekeepers over the din of the spectators.

50. A metal circus tent pole was being erected with the help of one of the circus elephants when it touched a high voltage power line that was overhead. The surge of electricity killed the elephant, whose body fell onto the trainer who was directing the activity, killing him.

51. The "heavily armed man" was a muscular weight lifter participating in the Olympics. His success at a variety of weight-lifting events (holding up several "bars") had robbed other contestants of their chance for gold or silver medals.

52. The woman was playing Monopoly® with some friends. She rolled the dice and stopped her game marker—a little metal car—on the corner of the game board labeled "Go To Jail."

53. The robber wore a motorcycle helmet with a face guard that completely masked his features. However, he had not remembered that his name was painted on the back of his helmet, which victims noted and reported to the police.

54. A school for sky divers.

55. Cinderella is running away from the ball.

56. Ludlow is a not-too-bright criminal. While at the post office one day admiring his photo on a wanted poster, he noticed that his name was misspelled. When he went to the counter to complain about the error, a plainclothes policeman waiting to mail a package became suspicious and detained Ludlow for questioning. He was subsequently arrested.

57. The photograph.

58. The barber is a woman, so she is allowed to shave herself.

59. Mac was the cook aboard a ship steaming up a piranha-filled tributary of the Amazon River. Not thinking of where he was, Mac reached over the side of the boat, dipping his hand into the river to rinse the blood off. The ensuing piranha attack did the rest.

60. The woman was in an advertisement for an amusement park. The woman was riding an attraction that raised a passenger compartment 200 feet (20 stories) into the air then dropped it back to earth beneath a parachute.

61. The pilot, a special type of ship captain, was guiding a ship through a storm-tossed channel when the ship's engine room flooded, causing the engines to quit and shutting down the bilge pump. The pilot ordered the passengers and crew to bail out the water from the engine room in order to restart the engines. Their actions were successful.

62. She was the quarterback of a football team. With the help of her teammates, she broke free from the guards of the opposing team and unsuccessfully ran for the goal.

63. As a judge, she has the power to marry people and grant divorces. This week had been particularly busy. She had already married two couples and granted two divorces, and she was engaged to perform another marriage.

64. The story is about worker bees becoming trapped in a Venus flytrap, an insect-eating plant.